Here I am,
    There you are,
        Where were we

By the same author.

The Right Way to Figure, Plumbing
ABCDEFGHIJKLMNPOQRSTUVWXYZ
Burn This

Here I am,
There you are,
Where were we

Tom Disch

Poetry Book Society

The Poetry Book Society Ltd
105 Piccadilly, London W1V 0AU

First published in this collection by
Hutchinson & Co. (Publishers) Ltd
© Thomas M. Disch 1984

Set in VIP Bembo by
D. P. Media Limited, Hitchin, Hertfordshire

Printed and bound in Great Britain by
Anchor Brendon Ltd, Tiptree, Essex

British Library Cataloguing in Publication Data
Disch, Thomas M.
    Here I am, there you are, where were we
    I. Title
    811' .54(F)   PS3554.18
ISBN 0 09 154871 3

Contents

Acknowledgements

These poems have appeared in the following magazines:
American Review, *Antioch Review*, *Contact II*, *Harper's*, *Jam Today*, *Kenyon Review*, *Little Magazine*, *Michigan Quarterly Review*, *New Statesman* (London), *Open Places*, *Paris Review*, *Poetry in Motion*, *Seshita*, *Times Literary Supplement* (London), and the *Washington Post Book World*. 'To Our Christmas Tree' and 'The Clouds' appeared in *Poetry* (Chicago). 'An die ferne Geliebte' was published as a broadside by the Bellevue Press

Here I am

Coal Miners

From my vantage in the company's office
I never cease to admire our coal miners'
Philosophic composure before the problem
Of faith. In fact I was one of the first
On our floor to fight for the right to wear denim.
I know it fools no one, exerts no claim,
And makes me look ridiculous in the eyes
Of Upper Management but how else, if I can't speak
To them directly, can I express my canine willingness
To let their Man be leader of the pack?
These small homages to the icons of his tragic vigour
Only allow us less guiltily to hypothesize his life
Underground: how he attacks the spangled earth,
Advancing slowly down its major arteries impelled
By an anger his own unholy din every moment renews.
His skin, like the limestone of a sea-worn cliff,
Has become one magnificent callus. His lungs
Are more dense with death than any cowboy's,
Whatever his cigarette. Because he has inhabited
Even this depth of darkness with the light
Of a common purpose his soul is socialized
To a degree we can but dimly imagine. Let us at least
Do that. Let us honour the dowdy churches
And ephemeral pornography that allow him to breed
Responsive sons who'll carry on the ruinous fight
With the first terrific lunges of a man's whole strength.
Let us wear, if only in our bedrooms or on certain
Holidays, a lantern on our heads in honour
Of his conquest of despair. Dare we suppose that ours
Is larger? But as for approaching him
In friendship, as for asking him to recognize
That by signing his paychecks in sanctioned simulation
Of the boss's signature we can be useful too –
No, that won't do. If they could hear us maundering
In the fictive caverns of our mirrored bars,
They'd only damn our condescending eyes.
Our kindnesses to them must be invisible or so discreet
As to seem so: building the movies that let them dream
Of houseboats, spies in helicopters, just desserts,

Of Samson as he detonates the jet-black pillars
Of one subterranean temple after another,
Then carts away their shattered Baals
To be burned in a million benevolent mills.
This much we'll do, and more: for ravaged skins
We'll sell a soap and call it ever-springing Hope.
On Saturdays, between advertisements for beer,
We'll share their ritual brutalities and cheer them on.
But we must not ask to be imagined in return.
Our business suits and busy minds, disabling fears
And air-conditioned air, cannot engender
Reciprocal myths. Perhaps it is Virgilian of me,
But I'd prefer my brothers underground
To believe in their inalienable rightness.
I'd rather they didn't know too much
Of the contents of my desk, the source
Of my pride, the force of my imagination
As it gnaws at the dark walls that surround me.

Denver Airport

If we appear at such moments a nation
Of maniacs locked into fantasies all
As wacky as the born-again's hope
Of literally living after he's dead,
Perhaps it is useful. Perhaps
That paraplegic cowboy in the wheelchair
Simulating violence in the penny arcade
Is a kind of warning salvo to enemy hombres,
A skull-and-crossbones lovingly embroidered
On a sleeveless Levi jacket with, below it,
Our boys' motto, 'More Berserk than Thou.'
Such silliness *is* threatening,
Such willingness to pump adrenaline
Down the exhausted wells to force
Some last ounce of authentic energy
Up to the crazed surface of the eye.

And I, in my whitewashed shoes, am I
Less dangerous than other businessmen
Along this concourse? Are my desires
Less disorganized, my heart more sane?
Of course not: we're all monsters
Together, whose every smile reveals
A possible vampire. For now, however,
I'm content to feed my lazy id
Its daily ration of news as it oozes
From the airport's perpetual TV. No need
To turn to that girl seducing
Guileless travellers on behalf
Of her Hindoo god, no need to sign on
As a mercenary in the army of conscious
Reaction, no need to plunder, rape, or murder
When I'm so well supplied at every viewing
With the methadone of my vicarious crimes.
Why, only last night a man confessed
To a spree of no less than thirty
Killings, and when the amorous
Newscaster asked what warning he offered
The youth of the nation, he solemnly replied:
'Don't drink. Don't smoke pot.'

Another drink at the Timberline.
My plane's delayed an hour. The gin
Unlocks a benign tolerance for this land
Of languid, licensed water sprinklers,
For the brave rickety vans of teenagers
Going up one side of the continental divide
And down, like the fabled bear, the other.
It's all here to be applauded:
The purple majesty, the fruited plain,
The safe, soft air-conditioned bar.
Truly, I worry unduly. Most lunatics
Will accept a polite no-thank-you
In reply to their offer of a free LP,
Just as an umbrella suffices for most forms
Of storms. Tornadoes do happen, of course,
And the only answer's to get on your horse
And skidaddle eastward with a final fond
Yahoo! to the waitress who has been so kind.

The Forbidden Children

Ah, I still remember – can you? – when I began
To watch the war in Asia. My hair was down to my shoulders
  then,
And I had a 32-inch waist. The 'Six O'Clock News' would open
With this zippy, adrenaline yatteta-yatteta.
Urban violence was escalating, and everyone was
  simultaneously
Scared, indignant, and unconcerned. The basic idea
Was to try and look natural but at the same time bright:
Lots of appliqué suns and rainbows, and jokey slogans
Promising an easy lay to the world-at-large. Now
All that has disappeared. You can't go up to someone now
And kiss them or even start a conversation.
They've been innoculated against language; they're trapped
On the far side of some mental Iron Curtain, which the
  authorities
Forbid them to cross. But maybe that's not so.
I don't know. Maybe the problem's as simple as incest.
Maybe it's only natural for children to shy away
From wrinkled faces with puckered lips, to isolate
Themselves in the all-night acceleration of a revolutionary
Dance step, to drape their limbs in the latest taboo, fleeing
That look we never see in our own eyes, that hunger
To be young and callow and still entirely alive.

Manahatta Notes

Madison Square
Trees in bud, the traffic thin,
& the light Athenian.
Here sit I with three bags
of remaindered books, a New Yorker
all over again: ticking over
at double my London r.p.m. – fretful,
amazed at how cheap and how dear
everything is over here,

including the oldest friendships.
Nevertheless I've got to say
that in the arch-necessity of hope
New York deserves every song
we can sing to it. Walt Whitman,
Paul Goodman, welcome me home!
23 April 1978

Apartment Hunting

While ordinarily I quite admire the wolves
With whom I am acquainted – their sharp eyes,
Bright teeth, and invariable good humour –
I find it disconcerting, as a rabbit,
To learn that they're in charge
Of the Department of Safety and Burrows.
12 Sept. 1978

Prayer to Pleasure

Again! Oh glorious, I feel as though – Again
This wonderful sensation when I rub my hand
Against it: an effervescence of my very bones;
A bursting followed by a blessedness of peace,
Which I repeat at will. Tender oblivion!
Angel chorus! You ravishing, you glorious

Pleasure! Fill me past brimming with your glorious
Elixir! Excellent and only god, again
Destroy me with my wishes! Bring me oblivion
Perfect, eternal, entire! Come – give me your hand
Where jewels cluster like the scars of kisses! Peace
Be with you, and peace with me! Grind my bones

Into your bread, beloved! What use have I for bones
Or bread since I am blinded by your glorious
Periodicities? Before fermenting peace
Can turn to loss or need, I call to you again,
And you reply, my Pleasure, for ever at hand,
Never asking any price above that oblivion

I joy to spend my being in, the oblivion
Of delights endlessly reborn among the bones
Of sailors and their willing whores. Hand after hand
Was dealt them and they always played the glorious
Old game – eagerly too, the dears! Time and again
They won and lost and rest now not so much in peace

As in expectation of another piece
Of ass, another tug at the tits of oblivion.
When lunch is over, don't *we* hope to dine again?
And after dinner don't we save the chicken bones
For stock, thereby declaring faith in the glorious
Renewal of our appetites? To live from hand

To mouth – why not, since there's no other way? The hand
Is full, the mouth is satisfied, a perfect peace
Prevails. Ah Pleasure, it is you! Glorious
Provider! Sweet gushing source of my oblivion!
Drink up my marrow but return me to my bones
So that tomorrow you may suck them dry again!

Again I wait for you and place in your soft hand
These useless bones and scraps of meat, Prince of My Peace!
Bring them oblivion, Being most glorious!

Just Before the Cops Arrive

Something terrible has happened
but I don't know what. The letter
that arrived this morning will say no more
than that another letter containing the bad news
is on its way. It is something so terrible,
apparently, it can't be named.
Humiliating too, I have no doubt.
Today is Saturday. There won't be
another delivery of mail
till Monday morning at eight o'clock.
For one weekend, then, I shall live
the life of an escaped convict, getting

steadily more drunk and more hilarious
as the dragnet closes in.
Sister Fidelis used to ask what we would do
if we knew the world was definitely
coming to an end in the next half-hour.
High-tailing to church was not the right answer.
The thing to do, according to Sister Fidelis,
was to continue, unfluttered, at one's usual task.
Surely she was right. What better way to let God know
that one's conscience is clean? And mine – is it?
I believe so. Yet there is, for all that,
a sense of fitness to the nebulous but nevertheless
quite massive bad news, a feeling of
predestinate necessity that has less to do
with the symmetries of retribution
than with the fact that bad news is
ultimately inescapable. No matter
that we've reached another state, we're still
wanted men, on display at every jerkwater
post office. The letter may not arrive Monday.
A compassionate typist may have misaddressed it.
But even if I should never read it, even if
I should run away to Argentina, where they kill
anyone who prints bad news, it would still be there,
in its blue envelope, my own terrible truth.

Waking in a Strange Apartment

A table of walnut veneer, my second cup
of instant coffee, and three crinkly petunias
David picked in his brick garden to send over here.
I try to read my manual on motorcycle engines:
the clutch, when disengaged, allows
'an infinite degree of slip'. Some people
understand the way things work; the rest of us
just float along and trust to luck
and the good faith of our repairmen.
Ed is getting up. Today he finds out
whether or not he has leukaemia.   *3 July 1969*

17

Riddles

1.

I am this keenness and this edge,
The wager you can neither hedge
Nor win, the final sin, the wedge
To pry you from your window ledge.
Yet at the dawning of each day
See how gracefully I play,
Making merry and *distingué*
The face I would prefer to flay.

2.

Mine is a rhythm, a jangle, a beat,
That speaks to the innards and not to the feet,
And yet the essence I exude
Stops several calories short of food.
Oh scorch my bottom, make me steam,
And add who will a drop of cream.

3.

My song it is that saps the will,
Corrupts the mind, and robs the till –
So live with me and be my shill
And praise me for the very skill
By which I fuddle, fox, and fill
Your dreaming mind with all my swill.

4.

I am the silence that confounds
The possibility of any sounds
But those I've chosen to command.
I am the song a single hand
Can sing, compressing after and before
Into the Coda of:

5.
Although I talk of no one and
Of nothing else but me and mine,
I hope you will not understand
Just who I am until the line
Revealing all my taradiddle
As the substance of:

*(Answers: 1. A razor; 2. A percolator; 3. A television;
4. A score; 5. A riddle.)*

The Wounded Barbarian

Europe the second time is a rack
of postcards and a conversation
about money that goes on till 2 a.m.
Sidewalks, rain, a nonstop
Utrillo painting and the same
conversation continuing
past the fronts of shops that sell
nothing but postcards complaining
about this weather and the cost
of even the most ordinary defeat.

Concerto for Piano and Orchestra

*And these are not fairies? I was three or four times in the
thought they were not fairies; and yet the guiltiness of my mind,
the sudden surprise of my powers, drove the grossness of the
foppery into a received belief, in despite of the teeth of all rime and
reason, that they were fairies. See now, how wit may be made a
Jack-a-lent, when 'tis upon ill employment!
Sir John Falstaff, serve Got, and leave your desires, and
fairies will not pinse you.*

The Merry Wives of Windsor

There is no law but this: Do as you please.
It can be done! The orchestra agrees.
It can be done: the clarinet asserts
Its admiration of all rich desserts.
It burbles like a spring of Beaujolais.
It can be done – and shall be done today:
Into the mouth and past the rotting teeth,
Down through the gullet to the halls beneath,
To revel there like rustics at an inn.
Such fun! Heigh-ho! declares the violin.
Such fun, that instantaneously flings
Itself through sounding brass and trembling strings,
That claps its hands, and stamps its feet, and feels
The utter clarity of glockenspiels.
It can be done – and has been done today.
Now, once again! For what is flesh but clay?
And what's a life if not a shape to mold?
The mouth is timeless, neither young nor old;
The tongue within its morbid, damp concaves
Dreams of some sweeter world, forever craves
The milk of Paradise, the honeydews
Of holy bliss, the absolute good news
That God conspires in our blessedness.
This is the Faith all raving tongues confess.
It's only common sense (they rave) to make
Ourselves all lunatics for heaven's sake.
Beside an idiot who's mad for God
Every little philosophe's a clod
The raptured horns concur: the world's more bright

Beneath Faith's sun than by the feeble light
Of reason. Reason's so slow and, what's more, lacks
The inarguable logic of the Ax.
Come, kiss the Ax, and let its peace descend
Over this corpulent world without end.
A kind of march begins. The infant-kings
With lotus blossoms in their underthings
Storm down the aisles of history to seize
The day, and whatsoever else they please.
Too late the temperate piano sees
The dangers lurking in the likes of these.
Faith, though delicious on first plunging in,
Has this in common with the life of sin:
It leads to disenchantment when pursued
By those whose need is less than dire. Be lewd
As billyboats or get a gross tattoo;
Believe in any god that tickles you;
But be aware the day will surely dawn
When all of this excites, at most, a yawn.
Better (the piano thinks) to play it cool:
Plunge if you must, but use a swimming pool.
In sturdy fifths and octaves it commends
A quiet life of marriage and good friends.
Allow yourself to be deceived. The odds
Are that you will be anyhow. The gods
We worship are our neighbours in disguise.
By such deceits the path to wisdom lies.
Do what you should – and call it what you please.
The orchestra, disconsolate, agrees.

There you are

Ode on the Source of the Clitumnus

There you are, waiting for me,
Or someone, to praise you. Propertius praised you,
Carducci praised you – it isn't enough.
There you are, still, bubbling away,
Filled with more fish than Nature unassisted
   Could possibly contrive, and not three yards
From the highway – in short, a perfect sight.
Walden Pond, which I have never visited,
   Is said to be in the same fix – clogged
With cans and candy wrappers, alive with the jokes
   Of tourists who drive there with no good
      Idea of who this Thoreau
Might have been or why he settled in of all places
   This, but who all certainly must have expected
      Something a little nicer.

But wasn't the world always a mess – especially
   Just off, like this, Via Flaminia?
      Without wanting to lay asphalt
On the last living blade of grass, one may suggest
   That any beauty, over-advertised,
Inevitably perishes. Mont Blanc has not survived
   Unscathed till now: then could
      The Source of the Clitumnus?
No. You will grow uglier year after year
   Until no one will stop to look at you,
No guidebook will mention your name and poets
      Will have ceased to read
Propertius and Carducci; the Fiats and Peugeots
Will whiz by you in their haste to see St Mark's
      Subsiding into the lagoon.

But still you will persist to rise
Miraculously from the earth, and while you do
You must be praised. Every day the world
    Grows poorer as the population
Soars. There doesn't seem to be much time
    Until the likeliest holocaust prevails.
        Billions of us, at least,
Will die, and this fact already begins to seem
A little tiresome. So we are dying – haven't others
    Died before? Yes – and that's exactly why
We must praise the Source of the Clitumnus.
    Not that you are beautiful, not at all –
        But because you have outlived
Temples, highways, and religions, and because
    You are there, waiting for us.

An die ferne Geliebte

Oh Italy, my darling! So far away! So fair!
I'm back where I said I'd never live again –
    And you are there!

Your landscapes are Madonnas, your cities songs
That soar above the stone necessities
    Of getting on.

Oh loveliest of all the lives I've led,
Let me be your alien again, ravished by all
    I'll never understand.

Take me to your celestial skies! Remove
My clothes, my tongue, my eyes, and make a ruin
    Of what is left!

Resplendent! Honourless! Divine!
Sweep through my days, effacing them!
    Be mine! Be mine!

Ode on the Source of the Foux

The eye has reason to believe palm trees
    Superior to potatoes – but is it so?
    Is there more beauty in a chapel by Matisse
(I have not been to it, and do not mean to go)
      Than in some backstreet shrine
      Hallowed by a century
Of unassuming pain? Here in this once
Penurious hill town I find my own condition
      Writ large. I wince
    At the prices not so much because
I pay them but from the thought that I'm denied
      A share of the fleece.

      I hate the rich, and their police;
I hate the constant, conscious pressure they exert
      To keep me from their views –
      The seashores, mountaintops,
    And spiffy expanses that only money buys.
I long to live in a world I know cannot be mine,
      For they have it now
And mean to keep it as-is and all their own, selling off,
Dearly, only the cheaper bits: calves-foot, radishes,
      The thick mustard-colour pots of Vence,
The unskilled smiles of waitresses too fat
      To earn better tips elsewhere.

      You say I'm cynical. Not so:
I live, like all of us, in the world I firmly
      Believe in, the only world there is.
      I wear the clothes I can afford
And entertain with a wine that mediates between
      Absolute pleasure and total despair.
      I share, like the rich I envy and resent,
      All priceless superfluities
Of light and air, patterns of sight and of sound;
      I offer words, and think it big of me,
        As gardeners take pride
In the jasmine they plant, the birds it fascinates.

Meanwhile, of course, the source of the Foux
Produces its usual profusions of the stuff
   Tongues and bellies most insistently
   Require – freely, one might think,
     If one didn't look too closely,
   If one didn't sometimes visit deserts
And inspect the bank accounts of their residents.
     Nothing is free, *mon cher*,
   Nothing – not the light, not the air,
    Nor yet, *ma foi*, these words:
They were learnt at the cost of as many years
As these hands have fingers, or these eyes tears.

   You blame me, and you always will,
For reckoning the cost and measuring the flow,
For hating what I hate and knowing what I know.
   I cannot help it, and I cannot stop.
     The fountain's water
     And the traffic cop
   Have issued from a single darkness
     We neither comprehend.
It isn't our enemy, but it is not a friend.
   I drink its water, admire the flow,
    But it's getting late, and we should go.

For a Derelict

Nothing matters. You are through
Pretending you're a grown-up.
From the wreck of your life
There is nothing to save.

The strain has been too much.
You are tired. You are very tired. So tired
You are nodding off
Right on the corner of 5th and wherever.

From between your legs
A sinuous stream of beer or piss
Follows the course of least resistance,
The course you follow too.

Not even the angels who gather
Over the doorway of Citibank
To bathe you in their tears – not even they
Can make you behave.

You are tired.
Nothing matters.
We cannot bear
To look at you.

You Can Own This Painting for $75

In the velvet shadow of an elephant
A clown is crying. Tears big as pearls
Drop to the page of the Dostoevsky novel
In his polka-dotted lap. His own child died
Of leukaemia long, long ago. His wife became
A lesbian. His salary's inadequate,
All his experiences crushing. What living room
Anywhere could resist the icon of his smile?
Who, holding the fellow's skull to the light,
Would not wonder what thoughts once spilled
Through its sutures? Another glass of wine –
That's the only answer he will wink at now.
But listen: a trumpet! The elephant lurches.

Lost in the mists of her tutu, her torso
Wanders through terrible forests. Meanwhile
Her feet crush spring's first primroses,
Each step neat as a butterfly on a pin.
Now her hands are pinned to a windmill
And she is set spinning towards a new
Triumphant theorem: she falls, wounded,
Into its arms. Now the moonlight,
Like a fleet of cabs, circles the darkness
Where she hides. Throughout eternity
She will be thirteen years old: so
An evil magician has whispered to her shoes.
The poor pink ribbons glisten with terror.

Here is the world that never was,
Where we grew up, and there's the sun
Licking the green lollipop of a tree.
The zoo peers out curiously from behind
Invisible bars. Seals honk and lift
Their primitive eyes to the blue paradise
Above. Keep us, they pray to the light source
There, out of harm's way, for we have always been
Good children. Their grandmother will vouch
For that, as she rocks all day in an armless chair,
Making change and longing for six o'clock
When her son will come and close her eyes.
She can remember every brick of her childhood.

A Bread-and-Butter Note

Loyal, entertaining, well-to-do,
she perches with an independent grace
upon her husband's knee. His pleasant face
discusses English weather, art, the new
retrieval systems. Someone smiles at you
and offers cream cheese seasoned with a trace
of Grand Marnier. It is time to take your place
among the happy, healthy, well-dressed few.

Someone fills the glasses. Someone asks
a question you can answer. Someone smiles
at someone else. The ageless, golden masks
that ring the table in a wreath of styles
are undemanding as the miles between
the evening's mildness and the morning's spleen.

When Your Hand Shakes, When
Your Eye's Meat

When your hand shakes, when your eye's meat
In the lonely butcher shop of the mirror;
When every street's a corridor
In Home Town Jail; when you fail, and then
Fail again; when the lens of the door
Frames a stranger's weaselish face; when plot
Thickens and pace quickens and the
Graffiti won't wash off the wall;
When leaves sicken in the sun and records
Warp within their sleeves; when the weariness
Of many years claims another friend;
When pipes burst; when the first suspicion
Forms, when the hive swarms; when the poisons
Of the air plant their cancers in your flesh;
When no one answers, when the song exceeds
The breath; when the long-term trend of the market
Is down and stores are empty in the afternoon;
When you're transfixed within your room
By the squadcars' squalling rage;
When your hair goes, when your age shows,
When the cupboard's bare; when you walk
Along a gravelled path alert
To the hungers of lovers and squirrels
And the world for a moment flutters
Its skirts and you're able to peer
Into the whirlpool of your fear.

When Your Eyes Meet, When Your Hand Shakes

When your eyes meet, when your hand shakes
The hand of the salesman who sold you the hat;
When you land on *Go to Jail*
And everybody laughs; when someone's
Radio is blasting along the street
But you can't resist the beat; when you're all
Clapping at the Judy Garland Revival,
Or when you join the singalong at church;
When you stop to watch and have to give
The obligatory quarter; when someone's daughter
Or cat crawls into your lap;
When you happen to meet a friend
And it ends in dinner, when someone says,
'You're getting thinner', and you know
You're not; when the store closes
And the happy clerks herd you into the elevator;
When the TV implores you to believe
In something other people believe in
And you do; when anything's exchanged;
When a strange restaurant lets you use
Its toilet free; when someone passes
In a style you completely agree with;
When a dog scratches a door, when the first guest
Rings; when people, in public,
Kiss, or fight, or conquer fear;
And when you're here, with me, at home.

Ode on the Death of Philip K. Dick

God, if there is a God, and that is something
He could never decide, has thrown him away.
A dumb thing to do, you say? With so much juice
Still to be squeezed, with all that doom could do
To force new bloom from the pollardings
Of late middle age? He might have suffered much more.
Or he might, let us admit it, have got himself
A golden tan under the sunlamps of success,
Written his memoirs, and made friends with Leviathan.

This way he dies unreconciled, and we are left
With his books buzzing on our stained-pine shelves,
Their sting and sweetness frozen by the flashcube
Of his timely exit. *Finis*, he wrote, then wadded
Up the paper and swallowed it – though literally
That is exactly what he did not do. A suicide
Only by omission: he forgot to take the pill
His heart required, informing God, if He exists,
That He would have to keep it ticking by Himself.

I scarcely knew the man and have no right
To trim his obsequys with my romances.
There will be flowers from the studio that did
Its level best to level his best book
(But with, it should be understood, his blessing);
A special wreath, perhaps, from Harrison Ford,
Who (I'm told) he thought had meant to murder him:
Hollywood's latest, greatest star his murderer!
Lord, he had no need of my romancings!

And yet I'm sure he would have wanted them,
For he loved, as much as any 5-year-old, to hear
His story told – how little Philip all alone
Set off along the darkling road and won the love
Of Linda Ronstadt, or would have if she'd known
Him as we knew him, who loved him and still do,
Though only in the useless way we love
The newly dead. No, don't fret. Your story
Isn't over. We won't turn the lights off, yet.

What other things did Philip do? Were there
Giants that he slew? Dungeons where in chains
He languished? Were there witches and enchanters?
Did he dance on California's golden lawns?
Did his words assault the mighty, like the words
Of John the Baptist in Strauss's *Salome*?
There were. He did. But his words of prophecy,
Alas, were drowned by braying brasses,
Unheard by all our Herods and Herodiases.

Yet, as every poet knows, melodies are
Sweeter so. They are the honey ravens bring
To feast the poet in the desert of his heart –
Might-have-beens, imaginings, false starts.
For a while their wings will hover overhead;
Then, still unperceived, depart. Art,
In a word: art as the uniter of lobe
To lobe, of sic to non, of hick to city
Slicker; art as our reason for being writers.

Well, Philip, have I said it yet? The bitter,
Insufficient truth? I love you. It's not a love
To ease your feet from the concrete shoes
Of your completed oeuvre, nor yet a love
To warm your flesh or even earn you
Royalties. But let me say, for all your fans,
I love you, and I know that you'll return,
Our *divo redivivus*, each time your voice
Is summoned from the earth to tell its tale.

Easter Sunday 1982

An Address to His Soul
or
Donne Without Faith

Thou dear Soul, that hidest fellow-ferret-like
 From me, where hast thou gone now?
 Peek out and show thyself. Strike
Thy chisel tooth into my inattentive toe
  And make me spin about
  In delightful doubt.
 Rush from me and I'll pursue thee
Through our root-encorbel'd lair
  And out into the open air.
  Soul, beshrew thee,
 But I will undertake to prove
  There is no love
 So delicately labyrinthine
 As this, for thee, of mine!

Or if to see thee, Soul, is boon beyond behest,
 Let me only hear thy breath
 Enrich the cavern'd dark. Test
My faith with rumour of the imminence of death.
  Whisper in this ear
  And change my doubt to fear,
 My trembling flesh to a Crystal tun'd
To news of thy Eternity,
  Wherein to die is ecstasy.
  Soul, I am ruin'd
 And all my speech mere idle chatter,
  If naught but Matter
 Can exist. Yield, O Soul sublime,
 One word with mine to rhyme!

A Valedictory Ode to
the City of New York

Goodbye, New York! Glamorous Babylon, adieu!
All those claptrap musicals and midnight horror shows
Were true! But I'm leaving you anyhow,
    Gotham, for good and all.
You chorus girls and gangsters making Times Square *radieux*,
    Farewell forever! I'm bereft.
    Bojangles! King Kong!
The Jets and Sharks, and What's Her Face
    In *Broadway Melody of 1936:*
To the whole golden-hearted bunch of you – so long!

I can't take any more. They've won: the muggers,
The junkies, the welfare scum, and they're welcome
To whatever rare diseases their kisses may transmit.
    Let *us* vanish, lovely slum.
The moment they attempt to break and enter. We're gone
    Already! Nothing's left
    But the black dust
On their windows, the white dust in their veins.
    The joke's on them for having taken
Books they can't fence and don't know how to read.

But they aren't to blame (it's said): a larger greed
Devises these evils and bends their honest despair
To its own vile ends. Mere penury is not enough to make us
    Work at jobs we hate. We need
Fear. For this *they* were created – so that we'd live
    In daily dread of them, and of their
    Savage children more. Formerly
The hangman provided a sufficiency of public horror.
    Now his office is combined
With the lottery. Like Justice, Terror must be blind.

Is this unfair? Illiberal? I hope to heaven, yes!
They have our streets and wallets; must we surrender
Our respect? Ought we to praise their songs and dances even as
        Their knives are carving us?
If the gladiators aren't to blame, then is the crowd?
        I don't say, 'Kill them,' but I do
        Think they ought to be allowed
To kill themselves without our making too much fuss.
        My only regret is for you, my old
Metropolis, and what looks like your inexorable decline.

Rome declined, too, and who's to say the experience
Of being reduced to a swamp for several centuries
Was wholly bad for it? Here I am now, scribbling away,
        Feeling much more at my ease
Than I did a month ago on Sheridan Square. Rome
        Is all the nicer now for having been
        Through the wringer. There's a sense
Of crumbling, comfortable decay. And how was that come
        By? Why, when all the better sort
Of citizens decamped for the far-off suburbs of Byzance!

So don't worry, New York – you'll survive. And if you don't,
What difference, eh? You were never what you seemed
To residents, never the mere grid on which they fried,
        The schemes they failed at, the disparity
Between the stores they shopped in and their lives.
        You were their illusion, and mine,
        That human beings are basically okay.
And only need Miss Judy Garland and a sockdolager parade
        To keep us safely satisfied;
That even the Mafia will be decent, if it's paid.

You know what I mean – and much more! The way you smirk
As though to say: *He'll be back. I've heard this all before.*
I can recall how lovingly he brought the first fruits
        Of his innocence and laid them on the shrine.
He wanted *me to have them*, insisted *they were mine.*
        But when I gobbled them – the stink!
        They're all the same, these lads
From out of town. How eagerly at first they lick your boots.
        But when the next pair isn't to their taste
How bitterly they'll criticize you for your brand of paste.

37

Fair enough, and yet . . . I'm serious this time. The grand
Old lies are foundering. Priests snicker at their offices.
Children spray kerosene on Santa Claus, and all the while
        They know it's Dad. It isn't just
You, of course, New York. It's not *them* either. Nor all of us
        Tangled together. It's having passed
        A certain age, or point: the vertigo
Of all bad marriages when both parties reach the brink
        Of the precipice and gasp
At the disaster, distant but magnificent, in the valley below.

Where were we

A Catalogue

After the Tristan, walking past a row of posters
longer than all the Poussins in the Louvre,
or when you'd come behind me up a crevice in the rock
and the sheep I'd terrified jumped over your head;
Walking my father all over Tivoli, walking
in barley (as we afterwards deduced) and being torn to bits,
walking to Marilyn's when she wasn't there, or, secretly,
to Chip's hotel; Walking to the Delaware,
walking to Rodmell, walking into Italy;
Climbing the vast garbage heaps on Monte Mario
the second day of our fast, walking through Ostia
with Berna Rauch, through Ely when your lens was killing you,
and in the twilight, through Chartres; Walking with our clothes
    off
but not very far, walking down literally
into a cloud, walking over Brooklyn Bridge, walking dazzled
by the boutiques in the Montreal subway;
Walking five days in the mountains with 50-pound packs
and never once escaping the hordes of other hikers, never once,
walking to where St Francis lived inside a rock, walking
to Wordsworth's grave and the lovely teashop overlooking it;
Walking to Gloria's down Christopher Street,
walking on pavements that the leaves had turned
to glistening linoleum, walking in meadows
allegorical with cows, walking up various waterfalls;
Walking all over Paestum with a suitcase
and all over Pittsfield when its restaurants were closed,
walking home from *Buster Keaton Sulla Luna* and wondering
how it must feel to be world-famous and then no one at all;
Walking with groceries from Okewood Hill because they'd
    cancelled
the Ockley bus, walking for miles in anoraks
until the rain had finally defeated us, then walking back;
Walking in the Tuilleries, walking on beaches,
walking in all seasons, weathers, and degrees of appetite
everywhere I've ever walked with you.

Atocha Choo-Choo

For John Ashbery

The pie here doesn't taste
As though it were meant
To be eaten nor can I

Sir keep from the simple sweetness

Of seeming to mean
Something, the cheap
Shot of the easy

Deposit of block
A into slot
A, even as our train eases

Out of the station in a series

Of muffled collisions
Not so much discontinuous
As exhibiting a continuity

Apprehensible only to brake-
And signalmen, to whom
I might liken myself

At least insofar as I

Relates to U,
I.e., those signs above the two
Tracks between which we

Must soon choose.
Choose! Choose!
The astonishing shoes not of

Spanish but

Chinese women zip by our window
Suggesting several possibilities,
To wit: 1) None

Of this is real and we are
Dreaming; 2) the
Chinese cultural attaché

Has assembled the members

Of a traditional
Chinese dance troupe here in
Atocha station; 3) the more

Imaginative transvestites of
Madrid have hit upon
A new way to dramatize

Their estrangement from roles

Assigned to them by those who choose
Not to bind their feet; or,
Finally; 4) feet

Are to be thought
Of here in a prosodic sense
And these cruel

Chinese toeshoes represent

A needless tyranny – for see,
As the train picks up speed,
There are the happy natural toes

Of shepherds innocent all summer long
Of shoes, toes
That seem to say to us

We must choose if not them then

What they stand for, the
Freedom – or tyranny,
It amounts to the same thing – of

Nature, that primordial progressive
Educationist, ur-Isadora,
Whom even the arch–

Augustan Pope commends as

The infallible modiste.
We follow her, then, as we follow
U track through the cold

Castilian countryside,
Bleak with furze
Of the high plateau.

This will be a long train ride.

Delaunay's La Tour Eiffel

For John Berger

How it excites the sky itself,
Sticking up there to the amazement
Of all beholders. The clouds tumble
Out of the heavenly gearbox cheering
Hup-la! O Paris, nous t'aimons!
All that is lacking is a tricolour
Whipped to smithereens
By the prop of a biplane. Soon, I believe,
We will live all our lives in the air –
Circling the crystal earth
Like wireless messages, a throng
Of aerial mariners!
Fast as eyes can see, kinetic images
Will spread through the conquered blue,
And skilled mechanics coming home at dawn

From their buzzing aerodromes will see
You, glorious Tower, erect
On their bedrooms' electric walls,
Will fall asleep in beds
As modern as tomorrow morning to dream
Of riveters riveting rivets
In I-beams infinitely long. And this,
And only this, will be the future's song.

To Our Christmas Tree

Like the dowdy bridesmaid afterwards,
Conscious of the comparisons that can be drawn,
And that surly boy beside her in his rented tux,
And the photographer condemned
Through no fault of his own to torture newlyweds;
Or like the newlyweds themselves in later years
Trying to attach names and feelings to the eyes
That flash at the flashbulbs' glare –
We cannot blame you, Christmas tree.
Like them you're not responsible
For your sorry condition. Tall as you are,
I know you might have grown still taller
If you'd been left alone. Birds might have built
Nests in your branches – just think of that! –
And the wind would have picked your ripened cones,
A few of which might well have carried on
In the great tradition of your chromosomes. Instead . . .
But there's no need to tell you what you already know.
For what it's worth, *we* think you're beautiful,
And weddings are for parents, after all.

To Our Turtle

Paperino,
don't you know by now
you can't scale walls?

And anyhow
why should you want to
escape? You've every

reason to be
happy here. Few turtles
have an entire terrace.

Or such a
pile of lettuce every day.
Does Rosa make a fuss?

While you lie
helpless on your back,
she gets all the hamburger.

Can't you accept
your turtleness? Be like us:
proud of what can't be changed!

Yes, Let's

Then let's have a nice time together, forgetting
our feelings of

let's let forgetfulness itself climb the staircase to
the unlocked delightful room where we invent our own
Saturday afternoon

because neither of us had the time to learn to sing
on key. The nun would prod each black note with her long
wooden pointer and the class would quaver
along after

Yes, let's both ride our bicycles to the airport where
the wind has bashed whole trees down through the cyclone
fences and back into

feelings that were not at that time allowed
concrete expression

Alcohol Island: a Chronicle

The Jaws of Safety

Forget the past and make no plans.
While your seemly torso tans,
Plankton and planets swim and sink
And never feel the need to think.

Lift your eyes and still your hand.
Regard the sky, the sea, the sand.
When it is night the moon will map
Your way toward the waiting trap.

Serenade

To be enclosed by green and living things
    Among the songs of birds;
To sleep and feel the while awakenings
    Beyond the reach of words;

    To cease from dusk to dawn
To need or think; to sink into the ground
    And lie within the lawn
And see the moon, from night to night, grow round.

Sun and Sea

We went there for the season,
    And returned within a week.
There was no compelling reason –
    Just a general sense of pique.

It was hot – we knew it would be –
 And the beach was black with tar;
And we weren't all we should be
 At the fabled *Sol e Mar*.

Ode to the New Prices

Higher! and now higher: rise and astonish us
 Who can refuse belief to laws
As old as Archimedes', who stand about and view
 The ascension of the hordes
Of warrior balloonists and express surprise.
Surprise! As though we did not know
And hadn't seen it happening before our eyes!
Truth is beauty: so you're beautiful –
Absurd, pastel immensities that polka dot
 The boundless blue. You're brothers
To the finest paintings of our times,
 To Pollocks, Frankenthalers, Dines.
You are magnificent. Rise! Oh rise!

All that we thought we owned belongs to you.
 Like the first gods that men imagined
You require nothing less than our lives,
 And what could be more thrilling,
Really, than to fall a living sacrifice
Into the jaws of Moloch? O monsters sublime
As the floats of the best department stores,
Roll down our streets and let us hurl
Our children and ourselves beneath
 Your crushing rationalities!
Progress from neighbourhood to neighbourhood
 Devouring, till we are stripped
Down to the bright diamonds of our avarice.

Cosmology and Us

Assuming that 98% of it's invisible –
A matter, merely, of inference among
Such obvious salients as stars,
All the rest taking the form of black
Holes, possibly, or immeasurable clouds
Of ionized hydrogen – the following
Events (so some authorities maintain)
Will take place: where it encounters,
Far from here, the limits of all it can do
The universe will bounce backward,
Returning through and abrogating
Its earlier millennia until
It disappears into the singularity
From which it sprang. What happens is
What happens to an arrow reaching
Apogee: gravity
Jerks on the reins, and the universe,
Too tired to resist, retraces
Its footsteps to the big bang.
Suns suck up their dissipated energies.
Black dwarves glow red again. Novas
Surrender the planets they've incinerated,
Which, reborn, begin their long widdershins
Devolutions to the womb. As –
So tit-for-tat is this predestinating force,
So remorseless, so exact – will we!
Christ, for example, will be carried back
To Calvary, rehung, and left for these
Inexorable laws to resurrect. Already
His disciples will have been inspired to
Unwrite the words of their witness, while we
Of the twentieth century will long since have been
Disassembled into our ancestors' genes.
If only we had some idea of the likelihood
Of this scenario! A reversible life
Takes half the sting from death. Alas,
There is no means by which men of the future
May send us word of the world's slowing down
Or their recoiling lives. They can neither

Confirm nor deny their paradoxical existence,
For though they receive our messages,
These pleas and queries, all their answers
By the time they reach us have become
The message we sent out, reversed.
Useless to ask whether we'll die
Or be reborn into a mirrored life,
For the question erases itself even
As it is written. Forget the future, then.
Return to the Lethes of your childhoods
Where, loss by loss, you shall be gathered in
To the singularities of ever-dwindling loves.

At Various Times Today
– on Portland Road

At various times today – on Portland Road,
Where I was looking for my old address,
And then, experiencing no success,
On my way home – I looked at clouds that glowed
A glorious, unnatural pink. I ohed
And ahed and pointed at them to express
My approbation of a loveliness
So pinkly perfect. I quite overflowed
With admiration. The clouds sailed over
The streets of London, moving west to east
With a slow, smooth, inexorable motion –
From Charing Cross to Plumstead Marsh to Dover.
Invisible in darkness they released
Their waters in the waters of the ocean.

The Ocean

One only needs to give the ocean some thought and it becomes describable as a street of houses:

To point out the features of the waves one has observed, or that one may imagine having observed; such as, that this moves forward with the curve of a woman's slackly muscled upper arm, when flexed, while the next displays a broader sweep that seems to amend or qualify the message of the first;

To proceed, then, to those more extensive forms invisible to viewers stationed on the shore, knowable only to those who make their home upon it, as the varying convexities of hills are known to the feet of their inhabitants, not to the racing eyes of truckers on the turnpike far away – to the swells, their endless amassings and fallings away, their seeming immensity;

To agree, nevertheless, that on a truly oceanic scale such forms, the largest apprehensible to sense, count for less than a wrinkle on the ocean's smooth bright face; that to the moon, which is their proximate cause, nothing changes on that face as it for ever turns and turns away;

Let us confine ourselves, on this account, to our own sphere of vision, wherein all analogies are, literally, homespun – as though our theme had been, in fact, a street of houses, for what can be said of streets or houses on a global scale except that their number must be immense and their extent unthinkable? Returning, therefore, to our station on the shore, let us admire the colours that a given moment, at a given height, may yield:

The fissioning, amoebic blues and greens that lull the inattentive fisherman, defeat the wistful watercolourist;

The almost-blackness interleaved with these;

The skein of jittery white lines that seem raw light, quanta all but broken loose (these few threads remaining) from accidents of form and colour;

And, ah! the rose enamellings of sunset, the fleshy washes of dawn when all ocean has become one single worshipful limb demanding to be mythologized;

And *then* the dance among these basic possibilities, each curve of wave engendering, in conjunction with an angle of the light, some necessary and sufficient charm;

But beyond charm there is utility: let us, accordingly, appraise the ocean's varied uses, as:

That it supplies our stores with fish (concerning which we might here intercalate heroic catalogues of their generic types, together with vast menus suggesting how each may best be cooked and dressed);

That it provides a unique, convenient form of transportation and a bridge broad enough for entire cultures to cross without colliding, as land-neighbours do (though not unfailingly: witness the sequence from Pearl Harbor to Hiroshima);

Progressing beyond utility, it would be well to note the ocean's often dangerous periodicities, its riptides, whirlpools, tsunamis, hurricanes, and grand bashings of waves on cliffs;

A proper appreciation of which, in even their simplest forms, will require some knowledge of the ocean's inner mechanisms, the liquid clockwork ordering its waves, the ponderous hidden forms of streams and currents;

And now, finding ourselves, as it were, immersed, we may choose to observe the simple, satisfying destinies of all its denizens, which are, amazingly, not merely warm ovals of food on our round plates, but living beings supremely capable of, well, swimming anyhow, and of being anthropomorphized and, thereby, loved (though never, it must be allowed, to the degree our fellow mammals may be loved, since fish are such egotists);

Let us, at last, say what may be well surmised of the ocean's obscurest depths, and speculate about its origins, which must be, in a sense, our own.

Do this, and the ocean that will then exist within your mind will be a worthy brother to the ocean you surveyed a year ago from its pebbly and often so-expensive shore,

On which the light played with such virtuosity,

In which you swam until you had become too cold.

The Clouds

Do you see yonder cloud that's almost in
Shape of a camel? *By the mass, and 'tis*
Like a camel, indeed. Methinks it is like
A weasel. *It is backed like a weasel.*
Or like a whale? *Very like a whale.*
Then I will come to my mother by and by.

Coral and shells are heaped until it seems
That everyone is rich, until the dreams
Of millionaires are clothing for the poor;
The world appears as it appeared before
The age of iron or the age of bronze:
Silvery beaches and wide, golden lawns.

Above all, changing: Perfect lambs one moment,
Moses the next, hurling his decalogues.
Elaborate as the handle of a silver spoon
Endlessly lifted to the perplexity
Of your smile. Smiling, collapsing – soundlessly
Offering themselves and moving off.

Slowly they graze the mountaintops, slow
Cows wandering home to their sunset –
Mildly anxious, leaking drops of milk
Into the monumental snow.
Now it is dark. Instead of bells, a blare
Of traffic and the chink of silverware.

A mother, fecund as Tuscany, pleased
To represent something so basically human
That even city people offer it
The yearly tribute of a Christmas card;
And yet she wonders who she'll want to be
Tomorrow when her babies disappear.

Love, you say – you love me. Then you become
A patch of sunlight propped against a wall,
A warmth that vanishes by three o'clock,
A pattern scratched upon a pretty stone,
A thought, a Romanesque basilica
With turgid fables flaking from the dome.

Or words – crisp unambiguous nouns, and verbs
Passing before us at an even pace,
Unswerving, with an army's iron grace;
But lovelier than these, if less distinct,
Those adjectives that decorate a blank,
White, wide, and slightly terrified face.

A wound, perhaps, but I've forgotten it
As if it were a dream that had recurred
Throughout my childhood: something orange, or red;
A flower, or a terrible mistake;
Someone at a previous address
Who gave me mittens, or who gave me socks.

An inclined plane, a wheel, a water glass –
Half engineering, half a work of art;
A human orrery that duplicates
The simple motions of the lungs and heart.
But turn it upside down and it becomes
Confetti circling in a paperweight.

As food flows into them, inaudible
To us, in cadenced shrills, they signal each
To each: I breathe, I move away, I need.
I need. The plankton, every molecule
Of water and of air is shaken by
The swelling and subsiding of their talk.

From century to century, the gist,
The motive antecedent to the act,
The indecipherable sense of it,
Even this, slips; the serried surfaces
Are left, draperies for archaeologists
To number and, provisionally, name.

You: you are the cloud I never name,
The language that I cannot learn, the game
I neither lose nor altogether win;
Illusion of another world above
The world beneath, outside the world within.
I squint, I blink – but still I see you, love.